stir fries

stir fries

LANSDOWNE

Contents

Introducing stir-fries

Stir-frying is the most popular way to cook food in Asia. The technique originated from China and over the centuries it has been adopted throughout Asian kitchens. Vietnamese cuisine, for example, is a fusion of the best culinary elements of China's traditions, with its use of chopsticks and woks, stir-fried dishes and plethora of noodles. Today, stir-frying has well and truly conquered the world, and is used frequently by Western chefs and home cooks alike.

The beauty of stir-fried food is not just that the dishes are quick to prepare and it is an extremely energy-efficient way to cook. Nor is it that the most tantalizing aromas are released when the ingredients mingle and sizzle during cooking, although this is quite wonderful. Stir-frying beats all others simply because it seals in the flavors and nutrients of the foods and preserves their original colors and textures, making meals tasty, satisfying and healthy.

With only four of the most ancient and rudimentary implements—cleaver, board, wok and spatula—plus a source of intense heat, stir-fries are easy to prepare. The success in cooking depends on having all the ingredients ready before cooking starts. The ingredients should be cut into pieces of about the same size, and the meat and poultry cut across the grain (partially frozen meat is easier to slice) to ensure they don't become tough during cooking. The food is then cooked in a wok or frying pan with very little oil over a high heat, constantly turning the ingredients.

When eating stir-fries, serve with Chinese-style tableware—bowls and chopsticks—as these add to the relaxed ambience this style of cooking affords. Tea is one of the best drinks to accompany stir-fries—try the lighter green teas, and plain or scented teas with jasmine blossoms are refreshing—as they cleanse the palate to enable you to enjoy the characteristics of each dish.

As a method of cooking it's obvious that stir-frying has several advantages: the ingredients can be prepared in advance to make cooking time no more than a few minutes, the dishes are economical to make, and the quick cooking ensures minimum loss of nutrients. Since stir-fried dishes cook quickly, they should be cooked just before serving so they are fresh and piping hot.

Enjoy!

Electric wok   **Stainless steel wok**

Frying pan   **Cast iron wok**

The wok and other equipment

The wok is synonymous with stir-fries. The word "wok" simply means "cooking vessel" in Cantonese. Its shape has remained unchanged for centuries. Woks of carbon steel or rolled steel are coated with a thin film of lacquer to prevent rusting. This needs to be removed before a wok can be used. To do this, place the wok on the stove top, fill with cold water and add 2 tablespoons of baking soda (bicarbonate of soda). Bring to a boil and boil rapidly for 15 minutes. Drain and scrub off the coating with a nylon pad. Repeat the process if any coating remains. Then rinse and dry the wok.

Carbon steel, rolled steel and cast iron woks also require seasoning before use to create a smooth surface that keeps food from sticking to it and prevents it from discoloring.

1 To season a wok: Wipe the wok lightly with oil and place it over high heat until smoking. Immediately plunge it into hot water, then return to heat to dry. Wipe again with oil and repeat these steps three times. At no time should you use soap.

2 To keep a wok clean: Rinse with hot water immediately after use and scour with a plastic or nonmetallic brush. Never use soap, or you will need to season the wok all over again. Do not wipe dry, but place over a low heat to dry. Wipe lightly with oil and store.

3 To heat a wok: Because of the wok's conical shape, a gas flame is preferable to electric as it disperses the heat upward along the sides of the wok. Gas also allows instant regulation of the heat.

4 To cook with a wok: Always preheat the wok before adding any ingredients, including oil. After adding oil, rotate the wok to spread the oil evenly up the sides, then heat before adding anything else.

Electric rice cookers are rapidly replacing conventional saucepan cooking. They cook rice perfectly and keep it warm throughout a meal. A saucepan with a tight-fitting lid also produces excellent results.

A good hardwood board is indispensable for proper cutting and other preparations. After use, cutting boards should be scraped clean with the back edge of the cleaver, rinsed with warm water, and hung to dry.

A good cleaver cuts, chops, slices, shreds, minces (grinds), pounds, peels, scrapes, flattens, and otherwise processes every type of ingredient. A light cleaver is good for fine cuts such as shredding and mincing (grinding), and a heavy cleaver can be used for chopping through the bones in meat.

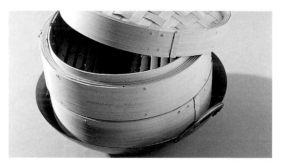

The two-level bamboo steamer is one of the cheapest and most attractive utensils for steaming. The open-slat base allows steam to circulate easily and efficiently and the lid lets excess steam escape through the tightly woven bamboo, with little condensed steam dripping back onto the food.

Mortars and pestles are essential for preparing traditional curry pastes. Their weight is ideal for pulverizing fibrous herbs and spices. You can use a food processor instead.

Electric spice grinders can be used in lieu of a mortar and pestle. Some have both dry and wet mix attachments. You can also use coffee grinders (keep one only for spices), but they do not have the two settings.

Wooden and metal wok spatulas or shovels are used for lifting and stirring foods in the wok. They have a rounded end, facilitating scraping along the contours of the wok. If these are unavailable, use any wooden or metal spatula or pancake turner.

Cooking chopsticks are a jumbo version of the smaller type used for eating. They are long enough for you to reach into a wok without getting your hands burned or spattered. They are useful for plucking, arranging, stirring, turning, testing, and otherwise manipulating various types of food.

Stir-fry ingredients

Today's cook can make superb use of an extensive array of ingredients. Each culture's culinary style seems to favor specific foods for its recipes. Basil, garlic, and chili are a popular combination for Thai cooking. The Vietnamese love garlic and coriander. The Chinese prefer a subtle blending of sweet and sour, hence the use of lemongrass, ginger, and star anise. The opportunities to create new flavors are endless—there's a whole world of ingredients to explore. Here are some of the ones we use in this book; don't forget to look at the glossary for more choices.

Bean sprouts These sprouting green mung beans are sold fresh or canned. Fresh sprouts tend to have a crisper texture and a more delicate flavor. Store in the refrigerator for up to 3 days.

Bok choy Asian variety of cabbage with thick white stalks and mild-flavored dark green leaves. Sizes of bunches vary, from longer than celery stalks to baby bok choy, which are about 6 inches (15 cm) long. Also known as Chinese cabbage. If unavailable, use Chinese broccoli or choy sum.

Cardamom This member of the ginger family produces pods that contain seeds with a strong lemony flavor. It is available ground, but for best flavor, grind your own just before using.

Chilies Fresh chilies are available in a combination of sizes and are either red or green. The seeds and membranes are the "hot" parts, so if you prefer less heat in your food, remove them before chopping or grinding. You could also reduce (or add to) the amount of chilies used in a recipe. Chilies are also available dried.

Choy sum Popular and widely available Chinese green with yellow flowers and thin stalks. Every part of this mild-flavored vegetable can be used. Also known as flowering cabbage.

Daikon This giant white radish, eaten in a variety of forms as an aid to digestion, is enormously popular in Japan and suits stir-fry dishes perfectly.

Galangal A rhizome with a sharp flavor, sometimes called Thai ginger, it has reddish skin, orange or white flesh and a peppery ginger-like flavor. Fresh galangal should be peeled before use, then sliced or grated. It is also available dried.

Top row: Bean sprouts, bok choy, cardamon; Centre row: Chilies, choy sum, daikon; Bottom row: Galangal, ginger

Ginger Thick rootlike rhizome of the ginger plant, a tall flowering tropical plant native to China. It has a sharp, pungent flavor. Once the tan skin is peeled from fresh ginger, the ivory to greenish yellow flesh is grated or sliced. Used fresh in sweet and savory cooking and beverages.

Kaffir lime leaves Fragrant, shiny, dark green leaves from the kaffir lime tree used fresh or dried, whole or shredded, for their enticing citrus flavor.

Lemongrass Pale stalks of a tropical grass that contribute an intense lemon flavor to Southeast Asian dishes. After the green blades are removed, the stalks are bruised or sliced before use.

Saffron threads If pepper is the king of spices, then saffron is the queen. Saffron threads are the dried stigmas from a variety of crocus flower, each of which produces only three stigmas. Harvesting saffron is labor-intensive, making it the most costly spice in the world. Saffron threads are generally soaked in a warm liquid to release their intense gold-yellow color and pungent, earthy aroma and flavor.

Shallots (French shallots) Resembling clustered tiny onions, shallots are brown, gold or pink to purple in color. The white parts of scallions (spring onions) may be substituted.

Shiitake mushrooms These are available fresh or dried. If dried, they should be soaked before use for 30 minutes in several changes of water. The stems are then removed and discarded.

Soy sauce Made from fermented soybeans and used to enhance the flavor of many dishes, different soy sauces have different tastes. Chinese soy sauce is saltier and stronger in taste than the Japanese style. Keep refrigerated once opened and use within 12 months.

Star anise Dark brown, star-shaped spice with a flavor similar to aniseed but with more depth and sweetness. It is the dried fruit from a variety of evergreen magnolia tree. Commonly used in Chinese cooking, star anise also makes an appearance in Indian foods.

Tamarind Tamarind paste and pulp are very sour. The paste, sold in block form, requires dilution in hot water and straining. More convenient is commercially available tamarind pulp, puree or water, sold in jars. Because there can be a difference in sourness between commercial and homemade puree, the quantities required are variable.

Top row: Kaffir lime leaves, lemongrass, saffron threads; Centre row: Shallots, shiitake mushrooms, soy sauce; Bottom row: Star anise, tamarind

How to ...

Chop an onion

1 Halve onion lengthwise through root and stem ends.

2 Peel onion by removing outer layers of skin.

3 Slice through each onion half 3 or 4 times, parallel to cut surface, to within ½ inch (12 mm) of root end.

4 Slice 4 or 5 times through onion, without cutting into root end.

5 Finally, cut through previous cuts.

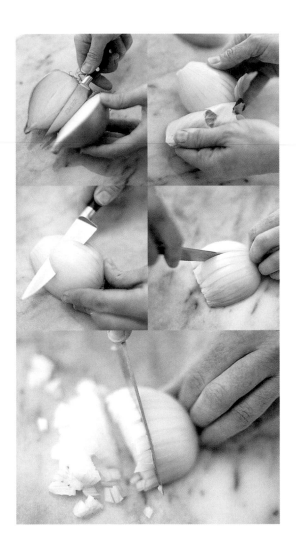

Chop fresh herbs

Use sharp kitchen shears to snip fresh herbs.
For fine shreds, roll several leaves together into
a tight cylinder, then slice crosswise. Tender
leaves such as basil and mint merely need to
be pinched from their stems.

Deseed a bell pepper (capsicum)

1 If recipe requires a whole pepper, slice top
  off with a sharp knife. If not, cut bell
  pepper in half through stem.

2 Using your fingers, remove and discard
  seeds and white pith from inside pepper.

Make a chili flower

Medium length chilies, either green or red, are ideal for the simplest of chili flowers. Make sure that they are very crisp and fresh.

1 Hold the chili flat on a board and use a thin sharp knife to cut lengthwise along the chili from stem to tip. Make about 5 parallel cuts just through the skin to the seeds, but not across them to the other side.

2 Plunge chili into ice water and the chili "petals" will curl back, while the seed cluster becomes the stamen. If parts of the flower remain closed, prod them gently with the knife and return the flower to the water. These will keep for up to 36 hours if refrigerated in cold water.

Long chilies do not blossom as exquisitely as the shorter varieties. To make this garnish, which resembles the beautiful kiriboon flower of Southeast Asia, use a scalpel or (preferably) a thin V-shaped garnishing knife (available at cookware shops and from some cake-decorating suppliers).

1 Make small V-shaped incisions along the length of the chili, in parallel rows. They should be about ⅛ inch (3 mm) wide and no more than ¼ inch (6 mm) long.

2 Plunge into ice water, as for medium chili, until the incisions curl back like a flower.

Note: For a more spectacular presentation, stick a thin sliver of carrot into each of the chiseled holes.

Prepare steamed rice

Though commonly referred to as "steamed rice", standard rice that accompanies most hot and spicy food is actually boiled. When cooked, rice swells to two and half times its volume. Estimate about 1–1½ cups cooked rice per person. If you are using an electric rice cooker, follow the manufacturer's directions. If using a saucepan, the steps are as simple as 1, 2 and 3 below.

1   Rinse rice until the water runs clear, but do not overwork the rice or the grains may break. Drain the rice and put it in a deep, heavy saucepan with a tight-fitting lid.

2   Fill the pan with water to cover the rice by ¾ inch (2 cm). Traditionally, cooks measured by placing their index finger on the rice, adding just enough water to touch their first joint. Do not measure from the pan's bottom, but from the top of the rice. Over high heat, bring the water to a boil and cook until craters form on the rice's surface and the water has disappeared. Immediately cover tightly and reduce heat to a bare simmer. Cook for about 20 minutes, or until tender. Do not lift the lid during the cooking.

3   Use a wooden rice paddle or wooden spoon to fluff the rice up and loosen the grains. If cooking in a nonstick pan, using a bamboo or wooden implement avoids scratching the surface. Serve immediately with your stir-fried dishes.

Appetizers and entrées

BEER BATTERED PRAWNS

SERVES 6–8 AS APPETIZER, 4 AS ENTRÉE

1 mango, peeled, pitted and chopped
1/2 cup (2 oz/60 g) chopped scallions
  (shallots/spring onions)
1/2 small red chili, seeded and chopped
3 tablespoons lime juice
2 teaspoons Asian sesame oil
1/2 cup (3/4 oz/20 g) chopped fresh basil
ground pepper to taste
1 1/2 cups (7 1/2 oz/235 g) all-purpose (plain) flour
1 teaspoon baking powder (bicarbonate of soda)
1 teaspoon salt
1/2 teaspoon red chili flakes
1 teaspoon brown sugar
1 3/4 cups (14 fl oz/440 ml) beer
3 cups (24 fl oz/750 ml) vegetable oil for deep-frying
20 jumbo shrimp (king prawns), peeled and deveined,
  tails intact
lime wedges, for serving

To make salsa: In a bowl, combine mango, scallions, chili, lime juice, sesame oil, basil and ground pepper. Mix well and set aside.

Sift flour, baking powder and salt into bowl. Stir in red chili flakes and sugar. Pour in beer and mix with wooden spoon until batter is smooth.

In a wok, heat oil until it reaches 375°F (190°C) on deep-frying thermometer or until a small bread cube dropped in oil sizzles and turns golden. Dip prawns, one at a time, into batter, allow excess to drain off and carefully drop prawns in hot oil. Deep-fry until golden, 30–60 seconds. Using slotted spoon, remove from wok and drain on paper towels. Continue until all prawns are cooked.

Serve prawns hot with lime wedges and mango salsa.

CARROT, COCONUT AND GINGER SOUP

SERVES 4

1 tablespoon vegetable oil
1 teaspoon Asian sesame oil
1 small red chili, seeded and chopped
4 cloves garlic, crushed
3 teaspoons peeled and grated fresh ginger
2 onions, chopped
2 lb (1 kg) carrots, peeled and sliced
1 teaspoon ground cumin

1 teaspoon ground turmeric
4 cups (32 fl oz/1 L) coconut milk
2 cups (16 fl oz/500 ml) vegetable or chicken stock
salt and ground pepper to taste
fresh tarragon leaves, for serving

In a wok over a medium heat, warm vegetable and sesame oils. Add chili, garlic and ginger and stir-fry until aromatic, about 1 minute. Add onions, carrots, cumin and turmeric and stir-fry until onions are softened, about 2 minutes.

Pour in coconut milk and stock. Bring to a boil, reduce heat to low and simmer, uncovered, until carrots are tender, 12–15 minutes. Remove from heat.

Working in batches, ladle soup into food processor or blender and process until smooth. Return to wok and heat through for 2 minutes. Taste and season with salt and pepper.

To serve, ladle into individual bowls and garnish with tarragon leaves.

CHILI-CHICKEN DUMPLINGS

MAKES 16

8 oz (250 g) ground (minced) chicken

4 scallions (shallots/spring onions), finely chopped

¼ clove garlic, crushed

¼ cup (1½ oz/45 g) roasted peanuts, finely chopped

¼ cup (⅓ oz/10 g) cilantro (fresh coriander) leaves, chopped

1 tablespoon sweet chili sauce

2 teaspoons soy sauce

½ teaspoon fish sauce

16 round wonton or pot sticker (gow gee) wrappers

¼ cup (2 fl oz/60 ml) rice vinegar

¼ cup (2 fl oz/60 ml) fresh lime juice

2 teaspoons fish sauce

1 tablespoon packed palm or brown sugar

1 tablespoon water

1 clove garlic, crushed

1 small fresh red chili, seeded and finely chopped (leave seeds in for more heat)

In a bowl, combine chicken, scallions, garlic, peanuts, cilantro, chili sauce, soy sauce and fish sauce. Place wrappers on a work surface and cover with a damp kitchen towel to prevent them from drying out. Take each wrapper and place in a gow gee press, or place 1 wrapper on a work surface. Spoon 2 teaspoons filling in center of wrapper. Brush edges of wrapper with water, and close seal of press, or fold in half, pressing with fingers to seal and make a frilled edge. Cover with a damp kitchen towel and repeat with remaining wrappers and filling.

Place dumplings in a steamer or steamer basket lined with parchment (baking) paper, leaving some space for steam to circulate efficiently. Partially fill a wok or pot with water (steamer or basket should not touch water) and bring to a rapid simmer. Place steamer over boiling water and cover. Steam for 10 minutes.

For chili sauce: In a bowl, combine rice vinegar, lime juice, fish sauce, sugar, water, garlic and chili. Stir constantly until sugar dissolves. Serve dumplings warm, with chili sauce.

CILANTRO AND LIME FISH CAKES

MAKES 36

1 lb (500 g) redfish fillets or skinless, boneless
   white-fleshed fish fillets
1 tablespoon red curry paste
1 tablespoon fish sauce
1 egg, beaten

2 teaspoons brown sugar
1 clove garlic, crushed
4 kaffir lime leaves, finely shredded,
   or 2 teaspoons grated lime zest (rind)
2 tablespoons chopped cilantro (fresh coriander)
2 scallions (shallots/spring onions), finely sliced
½ cup (2½ oz/75 g) finely sliced green beans
3 tablespoons vegetable oil, for frying
12 bamboo skewers
½ cup (4 fl oz/125 ml) light soy sauce, for dipping
lime wedges, and extra skewers, for serving

In a food processor, combine fish fillets, curry
paste, fish sauce, egg, sugar and garlic. Process
until mixture forms a thick paste, about
20 seconds. Transfer to a bowl. Add lime leaves,
cilantro, scallions and beans. Using wet hands,
mix until well combined. Form mixture into
36 balls. Flatten each to form a patty shape.

In a wok, heat oil over medium heat.
Working in batches, fry fish cakes until golden,
about 1 minute on each side. Remove fish
cakes from pan and drain on paper towels, then
place three fish cakes on each skewer.

Serve with soy sauce for dipping and fresh
lime wedges on skewers for garnish.

MISO WITH SCALLOPS AND GINGER

SERVES 4

8 oz (250 g) scallops, cut in half if large
¼ cup (1 oz/30 g) peeled and shredded fresh ginger
¼ cup (⅓ oz/10 g) chopped cilantro (fresh coriander)
1½ cups (12 fl oz/375 ml) water
1 lemongrass stalk, bruised and finely chopped
4 kaffir lime leaves, finely shredded, or 1 teaspoon
    grated lime zest (rind)
2 tablespoons red miso paste
1 teaspoon lime juice

In a wok, combine scallops, ginger, cilantro, water and lemongrass. Bring to a boil. Reduce heat, cover and simmer until scallops are opaque, 1–2 minutes.

Remove from heat and pour through strainer into bowl. Reserve liquid. Set scallops and spices aside and keep warm.

Measure liquid and add water to make 4 cups (32 fl oz/1 L). Return to wok and bring to a boil. Stir in miso, lime juice, and kaffir lime leaves reduce heat and simmer for 3 minutes.

To serve, divide scallops among individual plates. Ladle miso into small bowls.

SWEET CORN FRITTERS

SERVES 4–5

1 lb (500 g) potatoes, peeled and cubed
1 egg, beaten
¼ cup (2 fl oz/60 ml) cream
¼ cup (1½ oz/45 g) all-purpose (plain) flour
kernels from 2 corn cobs, about 2 cups (12 oz/375 g)
¼ cup (¼ oz/7 g) cilantro (fresh coriander) leaves,
    finely chopped

1 egg white
sea salt and freshly ground black pepper to taste
3 tablespoons vegetable oil
⅓ cup (3 fl oz/90 ml) sweet chili sauce, for dipping

Preheat oven to 225°F (110°C/Gas ¼). Bring a saucepan of salted water to a boil. Add potatoes and cook until soft but not mushy, 6–8 minutes. Drain well, place in a bowl and mash with a fork or potato masher. Allow to cool slightly. Add egg and cream and mix well. Stir in flour, corn and cilantro.

In a bowl, using a balloon whisk or electric beater, beat egg white until soft peaks form. Gently fold egg white into corn mixture and season with salt and pepper.

In a heavy-bottomed wok, warm oil over medium heat. For each fritter, spoon 2 tablespoons corn mixture into hot pan. Cook fritters until golden, 2–3 minutes per side. Remove from pan and drain on paper towels. Keep warm in oven.

Serve with sweet chili sauce for dipping.

VEGETARIAN SPRING ROLLS

MAKES 18–20

4 Chinese dried mushrooms
2 oz (60 g) cellophane (bean thread) noodles
   or rice vermicelli
2 tablespoons vegetable oil
1 onion, finely chopped
2 cloves garlic, chopped
2 tablespoons peeled and grated fresh ginger
2 cups (6 oz/180 g) shredded green cabbage
2 carrots, peeled and grated
1/3 cup (1/2 oz/15 g) chopped cilantro (fresh coriander)
1 cup (4 oz/125 g) fresh bean sprouts, rinsed
2 teaspoons fish sauce
2 teaspoons cornstarch (cornflour) mixed with
   2 tablespoons water
18–20 frozen spring roll wrappers, thawed
vegetable oil, for deep-frying
sweet chili sauce, for serving

Place mushrooms in a small bowl, add boiling water to cover and let stand for 10–15 minutes. Drain and squeeze out excess liquid. Thinly slice mushrooms, discarding tough stems.

Soak noodles in boiling water for 10 minutes. Drain and roughly chop into short lengths.

In a wok or frying pan over medium–high heat, warm 2 tablespoons oil. Add onion, garlic and ginger and cook until softened, about 2 minutes. Add cabbage and stir-fry until cabbage is softened, 1–2 minutes. Remove from heat and stir in carrots, cilantro, bean sprouts, noodles, mushrooms and fish sauce. Mix well and cool completely.

Separate spring roll wrappers, place on a work surface and cover with damp kitchen towel to prevent them from drying out. Working with one wrapper at a time, place on work surface. Using your fingertips, wet edges with cornstarch and water mixture. Place 1 heaped tablespoon filling in middle of wrapper. Roll up diagonally, tucking in edges. Seal edge with cornstarch and water mixture. Repeat with remaining wrappers.

In a wok or frying pan, heat oil until it reaches 375°F (190°C) on a deep-frying thermometer or until a small bread cube dropped in oil sizzles and turns golden. Working in batches, add rolls and fry until golden, 1–2 minutes. Using a slotted spoon, remove from pan and drain on paper towels.

Serve hot, with chili sauce.

Chicken and duck

CHICKEN SATAY SALAD

SERVES 4

1 cup (8 fl oz/250 ml) coconut milk
½ cup (5 oz/150 g) crunchy peanut butter
1 tablespoon fish sauce
1 tablespoon soy sauce
1 tablespoon peeled and grated fresh ginger
1 tablespoon palm sugar or brown sugar
1 teaspoon red chili flakes
6½ oz (200 g) rice stick noodles
4 cloves garlic, crushed
3 tablespoons fish sauce
1 tablespoon soy sauce
1 tablespoon minced lemongrass
   or 2 teaspoons grated lemon zest (rind)
1 lb (500 g) skinless chicken breast fillets, sliced
2 tablespoons vegetable oil
3 carrots, peeled and julienned
1 cup (4 oz/125 g) fresh bean sprouts, rinsed
¼ cup (⅓ oz/10 g) chopped cilantro (fresh coriander)
1 bunch mizuna or 1 head butter lettuce, leaves
   separated and trimmed
lime wedges, for serving

In a food processor, combine coconut milk, peanut butter, fish and soy sauces, ginger, sugar and red chili flakes. Process 10 seconds. Transfer to bowl and set aside.

Cook noodles, then drain and allow to cool. In a glass or ceramic bowl, combine garlic, fish and soy sauces and lemongrass or zest. Add chicken and turn to coat in marinade. Cover and allow to marinate in refrigerator 1 hour. Drain.

In a wok, heat oil over medium-high heat. Add chicken and cook, stirring, until golden and tender, 4–5 minutes. Add to satay sauce and toss.

In bowl, combine carrots, bean sprouts, noodles and cilantro.

To serve, arrange mizuna or lettuce leaves on individual plates. Top with vegetable-noodle mixture. Spoon on chicken and sauce.

Serve warm or chilled, with lime wedges.

CHICKEN WITH GINGER

SERVES 4–6

1 cup (2 oz/60 g) cloud or tree ear mushrooms
(black or white fungus)
¼ cup (2 fl oz/60 ml) vegetable oil
6 cloves garlic, coarsely chopped
1 small onion, thinly sliced

12 oz (375 g) boneless, skinless chicken breasts,
thinly sliced
1 cup (4 oz/125 g) loosely packed, julienned fresh
ginger, preferably young ginger
1 tablespoon fish sauce
3 tablespoons oyster sauce
1 tablespoon soy sauce
1 tablespoon soybean paste
2 fresh long red chilies, cut into large pieces
½ cup (4 fl oz/125 ml) chicken stock
8 scallions (shallots/spring onions), white part only,
chopped

If using dried mushrooms, soak in water for
10 minutes; drain. Use scissors to trim hard
core, then cut mushrooms into pieces.

In a wok or large, heavy frying pan, heat oil
over high heat and fry garlic just until it starts
to brown. Immediately add onion and chicken,
and stir-fry until meat is opaque on all sides,
about 2 minutes.

Add ginger and mushrooms, then fish sauce,
oyster sauce, soy sauce and soybean paste. Stir-
fry for 1 minute. Add chilies and stock or
water, bring to a boil, and cook for 1 minute.
Stir in scallions.

Transfer to a serving dish and serve.

Tip
If cloud or tree ear mushrooms are unavailable,
use an equal quantity of standard mushrooms.

CHILI CHICKEN AND VEGETABLES

SERVES 4

2 tablespoons peanut oil
1 small red chili, seeded and finely chopped
5 oz (150 g) skinless chicken breast or thigh fillet,
    cut into 1-inch (2.5-cm) cubes
6 asparagus spears, cut into 1¼-inch (3-cm) pieces
1 bunch bok choy, trimmed and large leaves halved
4 oz (125 g) sugar snap peas or snow peas
    (mange-tout), trimmed
4 oz (125 g) shiitake mushrooms, sliced
¼ cup (2 fl oz/60 ml) chicken stock
2 teaspoons soy sauce
1 tablespoon rice wine
1 teaspoon Asian sesame oil
crisp fried egg noodles, for serving (optional)

In a wok over medium heat, warm peanut oil.
Add chili and chicken and stir–fry until
chicken is golden, 4–5 minutes. Raise heat
to medium–high, add asparagus, bok choy,
sugar snap peas or snow peas and mushrooms
and stir–fry until vegetables soften slightly,
3–4 minutes.

In a small bowl, combine stock, soy sauce,
rice wine and sesame oil. Add to wok, reduce
heat to medium and cook until heated
through.

Serve hot, with crisp fried egg noodles if
desired.

CRISPY WONTONS WITH DUCK

SERVES 4

10 scallions (shallots/spring onions), pale portion
    only, cut into 2-inch (5-cm) pieces
2 carrots, peeled and julienned
1 Chinese roasted duck
6 cups (48 fl oz/1.5 L) vegetable oil, for deep-frying
16 wonton wrappers
1/2 cup (4 fl oz/125 ml) hoisin sauce

Using sharp knife or scissors, make 1/4-inch
(6-mm) cuts into ends of each scallion piece to
make fringe. Place scallions and carrots in bowl
of ice water. Refrigerate until scallions curl,
about 15 minutes.

Remove meat and skin from duck and
coarsely chop; discard skin if desired. In a wok,
heat oil until it reaches 375°F (190°C) on a
deep-frying thermometer or until a small
bread cube dropped in oil sizzles and turns
golden. Working with one wonton at a time
and using two sets of tongs, hold wonton in
taco shape and lower into oil. Continue to
hold wonton until golden and crisp, about
1 minute. Drain on paper towels. Repeat with
remaining wontons.

To serve, fill wontons with scallions, carrots
and duck. Drizzle with hoisin sauce and serve
immediately.

DUCK WITH LONG BEANS

SERVES 4

1 Chinese roasted duck
2 teaspoons vegetable oil
4 scallions (shallots/spring onions), chopped
1 tablespoon peeled and shredded fresh ginger
8 long beans, cut into 2½-inch (6-cm) lengths
2 tablespoons shredded orange zest (rind)
2 tablespoons mirin (rice wine)
1½ tablespoons light soy sauce
steamed white rice, for serving

Cut duck into serving pieces, leaving flesh on bone. Set aside. In a wok over medium–high heat, warm vegetable oil. Add scallions and ginger and stir-fry until softened, about 2 minutes. Add beans, orange zest, duck, mirin and soy sauce and stir-fry until heated through, 3–4 minutes.

Serve hot, with steamed white rice.

GREEN CHICKEN CURRY

SERVES 4–6

2 tablespoon vegetable oil
1 onion, chopped
1 tablespoon green curry paste or to taste
1 lb (500 g) skinless chicken thigh fillets, cut into
    thin strips

5 oz (150 g) green beans, trimmed
1¾ cups (14 fl oz/440 ml) coconut milk
4 kaffir lime leaves
1 tablespoon fish sauce
1 teaspoon grated lime zest (rind)
1 tablespoon lime juice
1 tablespoon brown sugar
2 tablespoons chopped cilantro (fresh coriander)
steamed white rice, for serving

In a wok over medium heat, warm vegetable
oil. Add onion and curry paste and stir-fry
until onion softens, 1–2 minutes. Add chicken
and stir-fry until lightly golden, 3–4 minutes.
Add beans, coconut milk and lime leaves and
bring to a boil. Reduce heat to low and
simmer, uncovered, until beans are tender-
crisp, 3–4 minutes. Add fish sauce, lime
zest and juice, sugar and cilantro. Cook for
1 minute.

Serve hot, with steamed white rice.

LARB SALAD WITH CHICKEN

SERVES 4–6

2 tablespoons sticky (glutinous) rice

2 thin slices fresh galangal

12 oz (375 g) boneless, skinless chicken breasts, ground (minced)

2 tablespoons thinly sliced shallots (French shallots), preferably pink

3 tablespoons fish sauce

2 tablespoons fresh lime juice

2–3 teaspoons chili powder to taste

1 tablespoon coarsely chopped cilantro (fresh coriander) leaves and stems

1 scallion (shallot/spring onion), including green part, coarsely chopped

1 tablespoon coarsely chopped fresh mint

In a wok or small frying pan over low–medium heat, stir rice until golden brown, 3–5 minutes. Transfer to a mortar and pound to a coarse powder with a pestle. Transfer to a bowl and set aside. Pound galangal in the mortar until pulverized.

In a medium bowl, combine ground chicken, galangal, shallots, fish sauce, lime juice and chili powder to taste; mix thoroughly. Heat a wok or large, heavy frying pan over medium heat and add chicken mixture all at once, stirring vigorously to keep it from sticking into lumps. Cook until opaque throughout, about 5 minutes.

Transfer to a bowl, and let cool slightly, then toss with ground rice and all remaining ingredients. If desired, garnish with additional mint leaves, and serve with vegetable crudités, such as cabbage, carrot, cucumber and long beans.

Tips

- Ask your butcher to grind the chicken, or do it yourself in a food processor.
- For Larb with Pork: Substitute an equal quantity ground pork for chicken, and cook as above.

PEKING DUCK PANCAKES

MAKES 15 PANCAKES

3/4 cup (3 oz/90 g) all-purpose (plain) flour
1/3 cup (1 1/2 oz/45 g) cornstarch (cornflour)
2 eggs, beaten
3/4 cup (6 fl oz/180 ml) water
1/4 cup (2 fl oz/60 ml) milk
2 teaspoons superfine (caster) sugar
1 tablespoon vegetable oil

FILLING
15 scallions (shallots/spring onions)
2 carrots, peeled and cut into thin sticks
1 Chinese roasted duck
1/4 cup (2 fl oz/60 ml) hoisin sauce
1 tablespoon mirin (rice wine)
15 chives
1/3 cup (3 fl oz/90 ml) hoisin sauce, for dipping

For pancakes: Sift flour and cornstarch into a bowl. In a separate bowl, whisk together eggs, water, milk and sugar. Make a well in center of dry ingredients, gradually add egg mixture and beat until smooth.

In a wok or frying pan, heat oil over medium heat, pour in 2 tablespoons of pancake batter and swirl pan gently to form a round pancake. Cook until golden, about 2 minutes. Turn and cook other side for 10 seconds. Remove from pan and repeat with remaining batter and oil.

For filling: Cut into each end of scallions with a sharp knife or scissors to form a fringe. Place scallions and carrots in a bowl of iced water and refrigerate for 15 minutes, or until scallions curl.

Remove meat and skin from duck and roughly chop.

Combine hoisin sauce and rice wine.

Lay pancakes on work surface and place 1 tablespoon of duck meat and skin in center of each one. Top with 1 teaspoon of hoisin and rice wine mixture. Add a scallion curl and 3–4 carrot sticks. Roll and secure with a chive, trimming off any excess chive.

Serve with hoisin sauce as a dipping sauce.

SWEET-AND-SOUR CHICKEN AND NOODLES

SERVES 4

8 oz (250 g) rice stick noodles
vegetable oil for deep-frying, plus 2 tablespoons
8 oz (250 g) skinless chicken breast fillet, cut into
    1-inch (2.5-cm) pieces
1 onion, sliced
2 tablespoons tomato paste (purée)
2 tablespoons palm sugar or brown sugar
1 tablespoon fish sauce
3 tablespoons lime juice
1 piece grapefruit zest (rind), 2 inches (5 cm) long,
    shredded
2 tablespoons water
2 tablespoons cilantro (fresh coriander) leaves
thin strips grapefruit zest (rind), for garnish
lime wedges, for serving

Place noodles in plastic bag and roughly break up into bite-sized pieces.

In a wok or frying pan, heat oil until it reaches 375°F (190°C) on a deep-frying thermometer or until a small bread cube dropped in oil sizzles and turns golden. Working in batches if necessary, add noodles and fry until golden and crisp, about 30 seconds. Using slotted spoon, remove from pan and drain on paper towels.

In another wok over medium–high heat, warm 2 tablespoons oil. Add chicken and cook, stirring occasionally, until golden, 4–5 minutes. Remove from pan. Add onion to same pan and cook until softened, about 2 minutes.

In a small bowl, combine tomato paste, sugar, fish sauce, lime juice, shredded zest and water. Add to pan, reduce heat to low and simmer, stirring occasionally, until sauce thickens, 3–4 minutes. Stir in chicken and noodles, raise heat to medium and cook until heated through, 1–2 minutes.

To serve, spoon chicken and noodles onto individual plates. Sprinkle with cilantro leaves and garnish with zest strips. Garnish with lime wedges.

TERIYAKI CHICKEN

SERVES 4

4 boneless chicken breasts
½ cup (2½ oz/75 g) all-purpose (plain) flour
2 tablespoons vegetable oil
½ cup (4 fl oz/125 ml) Teriyaki sauce
2 cups (16 oz/500 g) hot cooked rice
1 teaspoon sesame seeds, toasted
2 scallions (shallots/spring onions), thinly sliced,
   for garnish
nori, cut into fine strips, for garnish

Remove skin and trim any fat from chicken breasts. Place each breast on a cutting board and pound gently with a meat mallet to flatten slightly. Place flour on a plate. Dredge chicken in flour.

In a wok, heat oil over high heat. Add chicken and brown well on both sides, about 4 minutes. Remove breasts from pan and place in a clean wok with teriyaki sauce. Bring sauce to a boil, then reduce heat to low and simmer, covered, turning chicken three times, until cooked through, about 5 minutes. Remove from pan and cut into slices ½ inch (12 mm) wide.

Divide chicken among 4 plates with rice and top with teriyaki sauce from pan. Garnish with toasted sesame seeds, scallions and nori strips.

Beef and pork

BEEF CHOW MEIN

SERVES 4–6

6½ oz (200 g) wheat flour, rice stick
    or thick egg noodles
2 tablespoons soy sauce
3 tablespoons hoisin sauce
2 cloves garlic, crushed
2 teaspoons peeled and grated fresh ginger
12 oz (375 g) round (topside) or sirloin (rump) steak,
    thinly sliced
2 tablespoons vegetable oil
8 fresh shiitake mushrooms, brushed clean and sliced
6 scallions (shallots/green onions), sliced
6 oz (180 g) broccoli, cut into florets
2 tablespoons beef stock
1 tablespoon dry sherry
1 teaspoon Asian sesame oil

Cook noodles, then drain and set aside. In glass or ceramic bowl, combine soy and hoisin sauces, garlic and ginger. Add steak slices, turn to coat in marinade, cover and marinate for 30 minutes. Drain and reserve marinade.

In a wok or frying pan over medium–high heat, warm vegetable oil. Add steak and stir-fry until meat changes color, 3–4 minutes. Remove from pan. Return pan to medium–high heat, add mushrooms, scallions and broccoli, and stir-fry for 2 minutes. Add noodles, steak, reserved marinade, stock, sherry and sesame oil. Cook until heated through, 1–2 minutes.

Serve immediately, divided among individual plates.

BEEF STIR-FRY WITH CHINESE GREENS

SERVES 4

10½ oz (315 g) sirloin (rump) or round (topside) steak
3 tablespoons vegetable oil
4 cloves garlic, crushed
1 tablespoon peeled and grated fresh ginger
2 small red chilies, seeded and chopped

1 bunch Chinese broccoli or 6 celery stalks, trimmed
   and cut into 1¼-inch (3-cm) lengths
7 oz (220 g) sugar snap peas or snow peas
   (mange-tout), trimmed
3½ oz (105 g) fresh bean sprouts, rinsed
1 tablespoon oyster sauce
1 teaspoon sambal oelek
steamed white rice, for serving

Enclose steak in freezer wrap and freeze until slightly firm, about 30 minutes. Remove from freezer and thinly slice. In a bowl, combine beef, 1 tablespoon vegetable oil, garlic and ginger. Cover and refrigerate for 30 minutes.

Drain beef from marinade, discarding marinade. In a wok over medium–high heat, warm remaining 2 tablespoons vegetable oil. Working in batches, add beef and stir-fry until brown, 1–2 minutes. Remove from wok and drain on paper towels. Add chilies, broccoli or celery, sugar snap peas and bean sprouts and stir-fry until tender-crisp, 2–3 minutes. Add beef, oyster sauce and sambal oelek. Stir-fry until heated through, about 1 minute.

Serve hot, with steamed white rice.

CHINESE BARBECUE PORK STIR-FRY

SERVES 4

3 oz (90 g) cellophane (bean thread) noodles
1 tablespoon vegetable oil
6 scallions (shallots/spring onions), cut into
   1-inch (2.5-cm) pieces
1 red bell pepper (capsicum), seeded and sliced
4 oz (125 g) Chinese barbecue pork, sliced
2 bok choy or Chinese broccoli, trimmed
1½ cups (6 oz/180 g) fresh bean sprouts, rinsed
2 tablespoons soy sauce

Soak noodles in boiling water for 10 minutes. Drain and set aside. In a wok or frying pan, heat oil over medium–high heat. Add scallions and bell pepper and cook until softened, about 2 minutes. Add pork and bok choy and stir-fry until pork is tender, about 2 minutes. Stir in noodles, bean sprouts and soy sauce. Cook until heated through, about 1 minute.

Serve hot, divided among individual plates.

DRY BEEF CURRY WITH SWEET POTATO

SERVES 4

1 onion, chopped

2 cloves garlic

1 teaspoon shrimp paste

1 teaspoon ground cumin

2 teaspoons ground coriander

1 tablespoon chopped lemongrass

½ teaspoon ground turmeric

1 teaspoon ground paprika

1 teaspoon grated lime zest (rind)

2 tablespoons vegetable oil

11 oz (330 g) sirloin (rump) or round (topside) steak,
    cut into 1¼-inch (3-cm) cubes

1 cup (8 fl oz/250 ml) water

7 oz (220 g) sweet potato, peeled and finely diced

1 long red chili, seeded and sliced

1 long green chili, seeded and sliced

steamed white rice, for serving

In a food processor, combine onion, garlic, shrimp paste, cumin, coriander, lemongrass, turmeric, paprika and lime zest. Process until smooth. Set aside.

In a wok over medium–high heat, warm vegetable oil. Working in batches, add beef and stir-fry until brown, 3–4 minutes. Remove from wok and drain on paper towels. Add spice blend to wok and cook until aromatic, about 1 minute.

Add beef and water and bring to a boil. Reduce heat to low, cover and simmer, stirring occasionally, for 30 minutes. Stir in sweet potato and simmer, uncovered, until sweet potato is tender, about 10 minutes. (Add a little more water if necessary.)

Divide among individual bowls and sprinkle with sliced chilies. Serve with steamed white rice.

GINGER PORK

SERVES 4

1/2 cup (4 oz/125 g) sugar
1/2 cup (4 fl oz/125 ml) soy sauce
1 teaspoon mirin (rice wine)
2 tablespoons chicken stock or water
1 lb (500 g) pork fillet, trimmed of sinew, cut into slices
    1/2 inch (12 mm) thick
1/2 cup (2 1/2 oz/75 g) peeled and finely grated fresh
    ginger

2 tablespoons vegetable oil
2 scallions (shallots/spring onions), thinly sliced
1 teaspoon sesame seeds, for garnish

In a small saucepan over medium–high heat, combine sugar, soy sauce, mirin and stock or water and bring to a boil, stirring to dissolve sugar. Remove sauce from heat and set aside.

Dip both sides of each pork slice into grated ginger. Reserve any leftover ginger. In a wok, heat oil over medium–high heat. Add pork and fry, turning once until pork is no longer pink, 3–4 minutes. Add sauce to pan with any remaining grated ginger and bring to a boil. Reduce heat to low and simmer for 1 minute. Remove pork from pan and divide among 4 warmed plates. Spoon any remaining sauce from pan over slices. Garnish with sliced scallions and sprinkle with sesame seeds. Serve immediately.

PORK AND LIME PATTIES

SERVES 4

8 oz (250 g) ground (minced) pork

2 teaspoons fish sauce

1 teaspoon oyster sauce

2 teaspoons sambal oelek

1 egg white, lightly beaten

2 cloves garlic, crushed

2 tablespoons cornstarch (cornflour)

2 teaspoon grated lime zest (rind)

4 kaffir lime leaves, shredded

¼ cup (1 oz/30 g) chopped scallions (shallots/spring onions)

½ cup (4 fl oz/125 ml) vegetable oil, for frying

sweet chili sauce, for serving

In a bowl, combine pork, fish sauce, oyster sauce, sambal oelek and egg white. Mix well. Add garlic, cornstarch, lime zest, lime leaves and scallions. Using moistened hands, mix until well combined. Divide mixture into 16 pieces and shape into patties.

In a wok over medium heat, warm vegetable oil. Working in batches, add pork patties and fry, turning once, until tender and golden on both sides, 6–8 minutes. Drain on paper towels.

Serve hot, with sweet chili sauce.

PORK AND NECTARINE STIR-FRY

SERVES 4–6

2 tablespoons vegetable oil
3 cloves garlic, crushed
1 small red chili, seeded and chopped
1 lb (500 g) pork fillet, thinly sliced
1 bunch choy sum or spinach, trimmed and
     cut into 1¼-inch (3-cm) lengths
3 kaffir lime leaves, shredded
2½ tablespoons light soy sauce
2 teaspoons lime juice
2 firm nectarines, pitted and sliced
steamed white rice, for serving

In a wok over medium–high heat, warm
vegetable oil. Add garlic and chili and stir-fry
until aromatic, about 1 minute. Add pork, choy
sum or spinach and lime leaves and stir-fry
until pork changes color, 3–4 minutes. Add soy
sauce, lime juice and nectarines and stir-fry
until heated through, 1–2 minutes.

Serve hot, with steamed white rice.

PUMPKIN WITH PORK

SERVES 4–6

⅓ cup (3 fl oz/90 ml) vegetable oil
9 cloves garlic, crushed
1 lb (500 g) pumpkin or squash, peeled, seeded and
 thinly sliced
½ cup (4 fl oz/125 ml) chicken stock or water
12 oz (375 g) boneless pork loin, cut into thin strips
¼ cup (2 fl oz/60 ml) fish sauce
2 eggs, lightly beaten
fresh sweet Thai basil leaves, for garnish

In a wok or large, heavy frying pan, heat oil
over medium–high heat. Add garlic, pumpkin
or squash, and chicken stock or water. Bring to
a boil.

Add pork, reduce heat, and simmer until
meat is opaque throughout and pumpkin or
squash is tender, about 5 minutes. Add fish
sauce, then stir in eggs to just bind sauce.
Transfer to a serving dish, garnish with basil
leaves and serve.

Tip
For a spectacular presentation, serve this dish
in a hollowed-out pumpkin.

SALT BULGOGI

SERVES 4

½ cup (4 fl oz/125 ml) pear juice or ½ cup
    (4 oz/125 g) grated pear (preferably nashi)
3 tablespoons Korean rice wine
2 lb (1 kg) beef tenderloin or scotch fillet
2 tablespoons table salt
3 tablespoons sugar
3 tablespoons finely chopped scallions
    (shallots/spring onions)
2 tablespoons crushed garlic
1 tablespoon pan-toasted, ground sesame seeds
freshly ground black pepper to taste
3 tablespoons sesame oil
1 scallion (shallot/spring onion)
1 fresh red chili
shiso leaves or lettuce leaves, for serving

Combine pear juice and rice wine in a medium glass or ceramic bowl. Slice beef into strips ¼ inch (6 mm) thick. Add to bowl and let stand for 30 minutes.

Combine salt, sugar, scallions, garlic, sesame seeds, salt, pepper and sesame oil in a large glass or ceramic bowl.

Drain beef, add to marinade and mix well. Cover and refrigerate to marinate for 2–3 hours.

Cut scallion into 1½-inch (4-cm) sections, then slice lengthwise into very thin strips. Place in a bowl of cold water for a few seconds, then drain. Slice chili in half lengthwise, remove seeds and membrane and slice into thin strips.

Heat broiler (grill). Remove beef strips from marinade and broil (grill) to the desired tenderness.

Arrange shiso leaves on plates. Place beef on leaves, sprinkle with scallion and chili strips, and serve with steamed rice.

Tip
As Salt bulgogi does not have any sauce, drizzle with a little sesame oil to give it a sheen.

STIR-FRIED BEEF WITH EGGS

SERVES 4

8 oz (250 g) egg noodles
4 tablespoons vegetable oil
3 cloves garlic, crushed
¼ cup (1 oz/30 g) chopped scallions
    (shallots/green onions)
8 oz (250 g) lean ground (minced) beef
3 tablespoons water
1 tablespoon soy sauce
1 tablespoon oyster sauce
1 teaspoon cornstarch (cornflour) mixed
    with 1 tablespoon water
4 butter lettuce leaves, trimmed
4 eggs, soft-boiled, peeled and halved
¼ cup (⅓ oz/10 g) fresh mint leaves, for garnish

Cook noodles as directed on package. Drain and pat dry with paper towels.

In a wok or frying pan over medium–high heat, warm 3 tablespoons of oil. Add garlic and cook until aromatic, about 1 minute. Add noodles and stir-fry for 2 minutes. Remove from wok or pan. Add remaining 1 tablespoon oil to wok or pan over medium–high heat. Add scallions and ground beef and stir-fry until meat changes color, 3–4 minutes. Add water, soy and oyster sauces and noodles and stir-fry for 3 minutes. Stir in cornstarch and water and cook, stirring, until sauce thickens, about 2 minutes.

To serve, arrange lettuce leaves on individual plates. Spoon beef and noodles on top. Garnish with egg halves and mint leaves. Serve immediately.

Seafood

BRAISED SHRIMP IN GINGER-COCONUT SAUCE

SERVES 4

2 tablespoons peeled and grated fresh ginger

4 cloves garlic, crushed

1 tablespoon ground turmeric

1 small red chili, seeded and chopped

2 tablespoons white vinegar

2 tablespoons peanut oil

2 onions, chopped

1 lb (500 g) jumbo shrimp (king prawns), peeled and deveined, tails intact

2 tomatoes, chopped

3/4 cup (6 fl oz/180 ml) coconut milk

2 teaspoons cracked black pepper

2 tablespoons chopped fresh cilantro (coriander)

1/4 cup (1/4 oz/7 g) small whole cilantro (coriander) leaves, for garnish

In a food processor or blender, combine ginger, garlic, turmeric, chili and vinegar. Process to form paste.

In a wok over medium-high heat, warm peanut oil. Add onions and spice paste and stir-fry until onions soften, 2–3 minutes. Add shrimp and stir-fry until shrimp change color, 3–4 minutes. Stir in tomatoes and cook until soft, about 2 minutes. Add coconut milk, reduce heat to low, cover and simmer until sauce thickens slightly and shrimp are tender, 6–8 minutes. Stir in pepper and chopped cilantro.

Serve hot, garnished with cilantro leaves.

CHA CA FISH WITH TURMERIC

SERVES 4

3 tablespoons ground turmeric, or a 3-inch (7.5-cm) knob fresh turmeric, peeled and chopped

1-inch (2.5-cm) knob fresh galangal or ginger, peeled

1–2 fresh long red chilies, seeded

2 tablespoons fish sauce

¼ cup (2 fl oz/60 ml) water

1 tablespoon rice vinegar or distilled white vinegar

1 tablespoon sugar, or more to taste

1 lb (500 g) skinless catfish fillets (if unavailable, use trout, pike or salmon), cut into bite-sized pieces

5-oz (150-g) packet dried rice vermicelli (bun), softened and cut into manageable lengths for serving

¼ cup (2 fl oz/60 ml) vegetable oil

1 bunch dill, stemmed and cut into 1½-inch (4-cm) lengths

4 scallions (shallots/spring onions), including green parts, coarsely chopped

½ cup (2 oz/60 g) thinly sliced brown or pink shallots (French shallots)

2 cloves garlic, thinly sliced

⅓ cup (2 oz/60 g) chopped peanuts, lightly toasted

In a mortar, using a pestle, pound turmeric, galangal and chili to a paste. Alternatively, process in a blender or food processor. Add fish sauce, water, vinegar and sugar and stir until dissolved. Pour into a bowl. Add fish, toss to coat, and refrigerate for 3 hours.

Transfer fish to a plate, scrape off marinade and reserve, and pat fish dry with paper towels.

In a wok, heat oil over medium–high heat until surface shimmers. Add fish, a few pieces at a time, to hot oil, stirring carefully so as not to break up pieces. Cook until flaky to the touch but not crisp, 1–3 minutes. Using a skimmer, transfer to a platter. Repeat with remaining fish. Reduce heat to medium, add dill and scallions to pan, and stir-fry just until wilted. Place these on top of cooked fish. Quickly stir-fry shallots and garlic in same pan, with any reserved marinade, and spoon on top. Finally, top with crushed peanuts.

CRAB WITH YELLOW CURRY POWDER

SERVES 4–6

1½ lb (750 g) cooked or raw crab in the shell
1 cup (8 fl oz/250 ml) evaporated milk
1 egg, beaten
2 tablespoons soy sauce
½ teaspoon granulated (white) sugar
½ cup (4 fl oz/125 ml) strained chili oil (see page oo)
  or ¼ cup chili oil with ¼ cup vegetable oil
1 teaspoon curry powder
¼ cup (2 fl oz/60 ml) vegetable oil
1 fresh long red chili, cut into strips
4 scallions (shallots/spring onions), coarsely chopped
¼ cup (1 oz/30 g) coarsely chopped Chinese
  or regular celery

Clean crab by pulling off the apron flap on the bottom of the shell. Pry off top shell, remove gills, intestines and mouth parts. Cut small crabs in half, large crabs into eight pieces. Twist off claws. Refrigerate until ready to use.

In a medium bowl, combine milk, egg, soy sauce, sugar, chili oil and curry powder; whisk to blend well.

In a wok or large, heavy frying pan over high heat, heat vegetable oil. Add milk mixture and bring to a boil, stirring constantly. Add crab and cook for 2 minutes, then turn off heat and add chili, scallions and celery. Spoon into a deep serving dish and serve.

Tip
For a less piquant dish, replace half the chili oil with vegetable oil and use a mild curry powder.

GINGER FISH IN NORI WRAPPER

SERVES 4

¼ cup (2 fl oz/60 ml) shaoxing wine or dry sherry
¼ cup (2 fl oz/60 ml) light soy sauce
1 tablespoon fish sauce
1 teaspoon Asian sesame oil
4 fish fillets (snapper, bream, perch, salmon), about
    6 oz (180 g) each, and 5–6 inches (12–15 cm) long
8 scallions (shallots/spring onions)
4 sheets toasted nori (yaki-nori or toasted seaweed)
½ red bell pepper (capsicum), seeded and thinly
    sliced
3 tablespoons Japanese pickled ginger

Mix wine, soy sauce, fish sauce and sesame oil in a bowl, and pour over fish fillets in a flat dish. Leave for 20–30 minutes, turning once. Drain, discarding marinade.

Cut scallions into same length as fish fillets, leaving some green top on. Lay each fillet diagonally across a sheet of nori. If nori is too big for fillets, trim to smaller square shape. Place 2 or 3 strips of bell pepper and slices of pickled ginger down center of fish fillet. Add 2 scallions, with one green tip and one white tip at each end. Lightly brush each side flap of nori with water and fold over fish towards center, pressing gently to seal. Fish and vegetable strips will still be visible at either end. Place 2 wrapped fish on each level of steamer, and cover.

Partially fill a large wok or pot with water (steamer should not touch water) and bring to a rapid simmer. Place steamer over water and steam until fish flakes when tested with fork and flesh is opaque, 5–8 minutes, depending on thickness of fillets. Switch steamer levels halfway through for even cooking. Remove fish from steamer and serve with remaining pickled ginger and steamed rice.

MUSSELS WITH GARLIC AND LIME BUTTER

SERVES 4

2 lb (1 kg) mussels
½ cup (4 oz/125 g) butter, softened
2 cloves garlic, crushed
2 tablespoons chopped fresh parsley
2 tablespoons chopped fresh chives
1 teaspoon grated lime zest (rind)
freshly cracked black pepper to taste

Scrub mussels under cold running water with a nylon pad or stiff brush and pull off hair-like "beards", discarding any mussels that are cracked or do not close when tapped. Place in a large bamboo steamer or steamer basket.

In a small bowl, mix butter, garlic, parsley, chives, lime zest and pepper.

Partially fill a large wok or pot with water (steamer should not touch water) and bring to a rapid simmer. Place steamer over water, cover, and steam until mussels open, 4–6 minutes. Remove from steamer, spoon butter mixture into each shell, and serve immediately with a tossed green salad and crusty bread.

Tips
- Substitute basil pesto for garlic and lime butter.
- Remove mussels from shells and place one or two on an endive (chicory/witloof) leaf, and serve topped with lime butter.
- Substitute shelled and deveined shrimp (prawns) for mussels.

PAD THAI WITH SHRIMP

SERVES 4

5 oz (150 g) thick rice stick noodles
5 tablespoons vegetable oil
4 oz (125 g) firm tofu, cut into 1-inch (2.5-cm) cubes
2 cloves garlic, crushed
1 lb (500 g) jumbo shrimp (king prawns), peeled
    and deveined, tails intact
3 tablespoons lemon juice
2 tablespoons fish sauce
3 tablespoons palm sugar or brown sugar
2 eggs, beaten
2 tablespoons chopped chives
2 tablespoons chopped cilantro (fresh coriander)
2 tablespoons chopped fresh basil
2 tablespoons fried onion
lemon wedges, for serving

Cook noodles, then drain and set aside. In a wok or frying pan, heat oil over medium–high heat. Add tofu and cook, stirring constantly, until golden, 1–2 minutes. Drain on paper towels. Drain all but 2 tablespoons oil from pan and return to medium–high heat. Add garlic and shrimp and cook, stirring occasionally, until shrimp change color, 4–5 minutes. Add lemon juice, fish sauce and sugar, stirring until sugar dissolves. Mix in noodles.

Push noodle mixture to one side of wok or pan. Add eggs and cook, without stirring, until partially set. Then stir gently until scrambled. Stir egg through noodle mixture. Add tofu, chives, cilantro and basil. Cook until heated through, about 1 minute.

Divide among individual plates and sprinkle with fried onion. Serve with lemon wedges.

SAUTÉED SQUID WITH LEEKS

SERVES 6

1 lb (500 g) cleaned squid (calamari) (see Tips below)
3 tablespoons fish sauce
1/2 teaspoon ground pepper
2 large leeks or 6 baby leeks, white part only, well
    rinsed
4 scallions (shallots/spring onions), including green
    parts, chopped
3 tablespoons vegetable oil
3 small tomatoes, quartered or sectioned
1 onion, coarsely chopped
1/3-inch (1-cm) knob fresh ginger, peeled and cut into
    fine julienne
1 tablespoon cornstarch (cornflour) or arrowroot mixed
    with 1 tablespoon water
steamed rice, for serving

Marinate squid (calamari) in 2 tablespoons fish sauce and pepper.

Cut leeks and scallions into fine julienne.

In a wok, heat oil over high heat and sauté squid for 1 minute. Add leeks, tomatoes, onion, ginger and scallions. Stir-fry for 2 minutes, then add cornstarch and water mixture. Stir well, then reduce heat to low, cover, and simmer for 3 minutes. Stir in remaining 1 tablespoon fish sauce. Serve hot with steamed rice.

Tips
- Do not overcook squid, as it becomes tough and rubbery.
- If using uncleaned squid, increase proportion accordingly. To clean, pull tentacles and head from the tubelike body. Cut directly behind eyes to free tentacles from eyes. Use two fingers to pull out plastic-like cartilage and innards, and discard. Rinse and reserve tentacles and tubes. If small, cut squid bodies in half or quarters, and larger squid into 1-x-2-inch (2.5-x-5-cm) pieces.
- To tenderize and beautify larger squid, lightly score inside of flesh with a sharp knife, making a lattice pattern. This works best with larger bodies, as small squid are thin.

SCALLOPS WITH ARUGULA PESTO AND SWEET POTATO PURÉE

SERVES 4

1 bunch arugula (rocket)
¼ cup (1 oz/30 g) pine nuts, toasted
¼ cup (1 oz/30 g) grated parmesan cheese
ground pepper to taste
2 cloves garlic, crushed
¼ cup (2 fl oz/60 ml) extra virgin olive oil
1 lb (500 g) sweet potatoes, peeled and
    cut into 2-inch (5-cm) pieces
2 tablespoons olive oil
3 cloves garlic, crushed
2 tablespoons vegetable oil
1 small red chili, seeded and chopped
1 lb (500 g) scallops, halved if large
1 tablespoon lime juice
lime wedges, for serving

Place arugula, pine nuts, parmesan cheese, pepper and garlic in food processor. Process until finely chopped. With motor running, gradually pour in olive oil and process until well combined. Set aside.

Half fill saucepan with water. Bring to a boil, add sweet potatoes, reduce heat to medium and cook until tender, 10–12 minutes. Drain, transfer to bowl and mash with fork or potato masher. Stir in olive oil and 2 garlic cloves. Set aside and keep warm.

In a wok over medium heat, warm vegetable oil. Add chili and remaining garlic clove and stir-fry until aromatic, about 1 minute. Add scallops and stir-fry until tender (do not overcook or scallops will toughen), 2–3 minutes. Remove from heat and stir in lime juice.

To serve, spoon sweet potato purée on individual plates. Top with pesto, then place scallops over pesto. Serve hot, with lime wedges. Store any leftover pesto in screw-top jar in refrigerator.

STIR-FRIED OCTOPUS WITH LONG BEANS AND SNOW PEAS

SERVES 4

1 lb (500 g) baby octopus

1 tablespoon light soy sauce

3 tablespoons vegetable oil

1 tablespoon dry sherry

2 cloves garlic, crushed

2 teaspoons grated lime zest (rind)

2 tablespoon lime juice

3 small red chilies, seeded and halved

5 oz (150 g) long beans, cut into 4-inch (10-cm) lengths

4 kaffir lime leaves, shredded, or 1 teaspoon grated lime zest (rind)

5 oz (150 g) snow peas (mange-tout), trimmed and sliced crosswise

Working with one octopus at a time, slit open head and remove intestines. Rinse and place in glass or ceramic bowl. In small bowl, combine soy sauce, 1 tablespoon vegetable oil, sherry, garlic, lime zest and lime juice. Pour over octopus, cover and refrigerate for 1 hour.

Drain octopus and reserve marinade. In a wok over medium heat, warm remaining 2 tablespoons vegetable oil. Add chilies and stir-fry until aromatic, 1–2 minutes. Add octopus and stir-fry for 2 minutes. Add beans, lime leaves or lime zest, snow peas and reserved marinade. Stir-fry until vegetables are tender-crisp and octopus is cooked through (do not overcook or octopus will toughen), 1–2 minutes.

Serve hot.

Tip

You may like to replace octopus with 6 x 1 lb (500g) squid bodies. Cut squid tubes in half lengthwise. Cut shallow slashes in a cross-cross pattern on outside of squid and cut squid into ¾-inch (2-cm) strips. Marinate and cook as for octopus.

THAI RED CURRY SHRIMP

SERVES 4

1½ lb (750 g) jumbo shrimp (king prawns), with heads
1 tablespoon vegetable oil
2 tablespoons red curry paste
2 cups (16 fl oz/500 ml) coconut milk
1 tablespoon fish sauce
1 fresh red Thai or Anaheim chili, seeded and cut into
   shreds 2 inches (5 cm) long, for garnish

Shell and devein shrimp, leaving tails intact and reserving shrimp heads. Wash shrimp heads. In a wok or large skillet, heat oil over medium heat and fry shrimp heads until they turn pink, about 1 minute. Add curry paste and fry until fragrant, about 30 seconds. Add coconut milk and fish sauce. Reduce heat to low and simmer for 10 minutes. Using a slotted spoon, remove and discard shrimp heads. Add shrimp to curry and stir over low heat until shrimp turn pink, 4–5 minutes.

Spoon into serving bowls. Garnish each serving with shredded red chili. Serve with steamed jasmine rice.

Vegetables

ASIAN GREENS STIR-FRY WITH SHIITAKE MUSHROOM

SERVES 4

1 lb (500 g) Asian greens, such as bok choy, choy sum or Chinese cabbage

2 tablespoons vegetable oil

1 red bell pepper (capsicum), seeded and sliced into strips

1 small red chili, seeded and sliced

10 scallions (shallots/spring onions), trimmed and sliced

2 celery stalks, sliced

1 lemongrass stalk, trimmed and chopped

2 cloves garlic, crushed

1-inch (2.5-cm) piece fresh ginger, peeled and chopped

6 oz (180 g) shiitake mushrooms, sliced

3 tablespoons soy sauce

cooked egg noodles or jasmine rice, for serving

Wash Asian greens well and pat dry with paper towels. Trim off root ends and slice greens into 2½-inch (6-cm) lengths.

In a wok or large frying pan, heat oil over medium heat, until oil is hot but not smoking. Add bell pepper, chili, scallions, celery, lemongrass, garlic and ginger. Raise heat to medium–high and stir-fry for 2 minutes. Add greens and mushrooms and stir-fry for 2 minutes. Reduce heat to low, cover and allow mixture to cook slowly until greens are tender-crisp, about 2 minutes. Remove from heat and stir in soy sauce.

Serve immediately with egg noodles or jasmine rice.

ASIAN GREENS WITH LEMON AND GINGER OIL

SERVES 4

1/3 cup (3 fl oz/90 ml) sunflower oil
finely grated zest (rind) of 2 lemons
1 lemongrass stalk, bottom 3 inches (7.5 cm) only,
    inner stalks roughly chopped

3 teaspoons peeled and grated fresh ginger
1 lb (500 g) mixed Asian greens, such as bok choy,
    choy sum and Chinese cabbage
pinch sea salt
pinch sugar
juice of 1 lemon
lemon wedges, for serving

Place oil, lemon zest, lemongrass and ginger in a screw-top jar and shake until well combined. Set aside in a warm place for 5 days so flavors infuse oil. After 5 days, strain oil and discard solids. Seal and store lemon and ginger oil in a cool, dark place.

Wash greens well. Pat dry with paper towels. Trim roots from greens and cut into 2-inch (5-cm) lengths. If using bok choy, remove dark outer leaves, separate younger leaves and trim ends.

Warm 2 tablespoons lemon and ginger oil in a wok or frying pan over medium heat. Add greens and stir-fry until tender-crisp, 3–4 minutes. Remove from heat and stir in salt, sugar and lemon juice.

Serve immediately, with lemon wedges.

ASIAN GREENS WITH TEMPEH AND OYSTER SAUCE

SERVES 2–4

1 bunch bok choy or choy sum, trimmed and
    cut into 4-inch (10-cm) lengths
3 oz (90 g) tempeh or tofu (bean curd),
    cut into 1/2-inch (12-mm) pieces
3 oz (90 g) enoki mushrooms, trimmed
3 1/2 oz (100 g) bottled baby corn, halved
1/4 cup (2 fl oz/60 ml) oyster sauce
1 clove garlic, crushed
1 teaspoon Asian sesame oil
1/2 teaspoon peeled and grated fresh ginger
2 scallions (shallots/spring onions), finely chopped
1 tablespoon sesame seeds, toasted

Put bok choy, tempeh, enoki and baby corn in
a large bamboo steamer or steamer basket.
Partially fill a wok or pot with water (steamer
should not touch water) and bring to a rapid
simmer. Put steamer over water, cover, and
steam until vegetables are softened,
3–4 minutes.

Meanwhile, put oyster sauce, garlic, sesame
oil and ginger in a small saucepan and mix
well. Place saucepan over medium heat to
warm sauce, 3–4 minutes.

Remove vegetables from steamer and
arrange on serving plates with enoki in the
center. Drizzle warm sauce over vegetables.
Sprinkle with scallions and sesame seeds. Serve
as a side dish or light vegetarian dish.

BUTTERNUT SQUASH AND LENTIL SALAD

SERVES 4

⅓ cup (3 fl oz/90 ml) olive oil

2 teaspoons grated lime zest (rind)

⅓ cup (3 fl oz/90 ml) lime juice

2 tablespoons chopped cilantro (fresh coriander)

½ teaspoon superfine (caster) sugar

ground pepper to taste

1 butternut squash (pumpkin), about 1 lb (500 g),
    peeled and cut into 1½-in (4-cm) cubes

½ cup (3½ oz/105 g) dried red lentils

1 tablespoon vegetable oil

1 small red chili, seeded and chopped

1 teaspoon cumin seeds

2 teaspoons coriander seeds, cracked

Place olive oil, lime zest and juice, cilantro, sugar and pepper in screw-top jar. Shake well to combine. Set aside.

Line large steamer with parchment (baking) paper. Half fill wok with water (steamer should not touch water) and bring to a boil. Place squash cubes in steamer, cover, and place steamer over boiling water. Steam until squash cubes are tender but retain their shape, 10–12 minutes. Add more water to wok when necessary. Remove steamer from wok and allow pumpkin to cool.

Place lentils in saucepan with water to cover. Bring to a boil and cook until tender (do not overcook), about 5 minutes. Drain and allow to cool.

In wok over medium–high heat, warm vegetable oil. Add chili and cumin and coriander seeds and cook until aromatic, 1–2 minutes. Add squash and lentils and stir-fry until flavors are blended, about 1 minute. Remove from heat and stir in dressing. Mix well.

Serve warm or refrigerate for 30 minutes and serve chilled.

CHICKPEAS WITH SPINACH

SERVES 6

1½ cups (10 oz/300 g) dried chickpeas
    (garbanzo beans)
4 cups (32 fl oz/1 L) cold water
⅓ cup (3 fl oz/90 ml) olive oil
1 large yellow (brown) onion, chopped
2 cloves garlic, chopped
¼ cup (2 oz/60 g) tomato paste
2 tablespoons chopped fresh flat-leaf (Italian) parsley
1 tablespoon chopped fresh mint
1 teaspoon ground cumin
1 teaspoon sugar
salt
freshly ground black pepper to taste
1½ lb (750 g) spinach
extra-virgin olive oil, for serving

Put chickpeas in a bowl, add water and let soak in a cool place for 8–10 hours or overnight.

Drain chickpeas and rinse well. Place in a large saucepan with fresh water to cover. Bring to a boil, cover and cook over low heat until tender, 1–1½ hours.

Heat oil in a wok over medium–low heat. Add onion and cook until translucent, about 7 minutes. Add garlic and cook for a few seconds. Stir in tomato paste, parsley, mint, cumin, sugar and salt and black pepper. Add to chickpeas, cover and simmer for 10 minutes.

Remove any attached roots and damaged leaves from spinach and discard. Wash spinach leaves and stems well in several changes of water. Drain, then coarsely chop leaves and stems. Add to chickpeas, stir well and simmer, uncovered, until spinach is cooked, about 10 minutes. Mixture should be moist, but not too liquid.

Serve hot or at room temperature. Add extra-virgin olive oil to taste.

DEEP-FRIED TOFU WITH VEGETABLES

SERVES 4

13 oz (400 g) firm tofu, drained and pressed
canola oil, for deep-frying
3 tablespoons vegetable or chicken stock
3 tablespoons mirin (rice wine) or sweet white wine
2 tablespoons Japanese soy sauce

¼ teaspoon sugar
½ teaspoon Asian sesame oil
½ teaspoon grated fresh ginger
1 large carrot, julienned
½ small green bell pepper (capsicum), seeded
    and julienned
½ small red bell pepper (capsicum), seeded
    and julienned
1 medium red (Spanish) onion, cut into thin wedges
watercress sprigs, for garnish

Cut tofu into 1½-inch (3-cm) cubes and pat dry with paper towels. Fill a large wok one-third full with oil and heat to 365°F (185°C). Deep-fry tofu until golden, 3–4 minutes, turning occasionally. Drain on paper towels. In a medium saucepan, combine stock, mirin, soy sauce, sugar, sesame oil and ginger. Bring to a boil, add vegetables and simmer 1 minute. Combine tofu with vegetables and sauce. Garnish with watercress and serve immediately.

JAPANESE SEAWEED SALAD

SERVES 4

1½ oz (40 g) hijiki (see Tips below)
4 sheets usuage (see Tips below)
boiling water
3 tablespoons vegetable oil
½ carrot, peeled and cut into thin matchstick strips
1 teaspoon instant dashi dissolved in 1 cup
   (8 fl oz/250 ml) water
½ cup (4 oz/125 g) sugar
½ cup (4 fl oz/125 ml) soy sauce

Wash hijiki well in a large bowl of water. Any dust and sand will settle to bottom of bowl. Scoop hijiki from bowl and then soak in clean water for 20 minutes. Drain well. Place usuage in a bowl. Add boiling water to cover and soak for 3–4 minutes to remove some of oil. Remove from water, draining well. Cut usuage into strips ¼ inch (6 mm) wide. Heat oil in a saucepan over high heat. Add carrot strips and stir-fry until softened, about 2 minutes. Add hijiki and stir-fry for 2 minutes. Add usuage and stir-fry for 2 minutes. Add dashi and sugar, bring to a boil then reduce heat to medium–low and simmer for 4–5 minutes. Add soy sauce and cover pan with a lid.

Cook for 20–30 minutes over medium–low heat, stirring occasionally. Liquid should reduce by two-thirds. Serve warm or cold.

Tip
- Rich in minerals and proteins, hijiki is a black seaweed that is available dried.
- Usuage is thinly cut tofu that is drained and fried in oil. Also called aburage, usuage is used in Japanese vegetarian dishes because of its flavorful meat-like nature.

MIXED VEGETABLE CURRY

SERVES 4–6

1 tablespoon sticky (glutinous) rice
¼ cup (2 fl oz/60 ml) vegetable oil
¼ cup (2 fl oz/60 ml) red curry paste
1¼ cups (5 oz/150 g) chopped eggplant (aubergine)
¼ cup (1 oz/30 g) pea eggplants (optional)
4 long beans or 12 green beans, cut into 1-inch
    (2.5-cm) pieces
½ cup (2 oz/60 g) canned or 1 cup (4 oz/125 g) fresh
    straw mushrooms, rinsed, drained and halved
½ cup (2 oz/60 g) coarsely chopped cauliflower
    florets
2 cups (16 fl oz/500 ml) vegetable stock or water
2 tablespoons soy sauce or fish sauce
4 fresh piper (beetle) leaves, or 2 cabbage leaves,
    coarsely chopped
7 fresh eryngo (sawtooth coriander) leaves or 6 sprigs
    cilantro (fresh coriander), coarsely chopped or torn
1 fresh long red chili, coarsely chopped
¼ teaspoon salt

In a wok or small frying pan over low heat, stir rice until golden brown, 3–5 minutes. Transfer to a mortar and pulverize with a pestle; set aside.

In a wok or large, heavy frying pan, heat oil over medium–high heat and fry curry paste, stirring constantly, until fragrant, 1–2 minutes. Add eggplants, beans, mushrooms and cauliflower; stir together well. Add 1 cup (8 fl oz/250 ml) stock or water, and simmer for 2 minutes. Add remaining stock or water and soy or fish sauce. Bring to a boil. Add remaining ingredients and ground rice. Bring to a boil, then reduce heat and simmer for 2 minutes. Transfer to a serving bowl and serve.

Tips
- You can also add 1 cup dried cotton buds or kapok flowers (ngiu) at the same time as the eggplant, and/or 1 cup chopped acacia leaves at the end.
- You can add ¼ teaspoon prickly ash (kamchatton) with the chicken stock.

STIR-FRIED CHOY SUM WITH GINGER

SERVES 4

3 tablespoons fish sauce

3 tablespoons water

2 teaspoons peeled and grated fresh ginger

2 tablespoons vegetable oil

1 bunch choy sum, about 16 oz (500 g), trimmed
and cut into 3-inch (7.5-cm) lengths

In a small bowl, combine fish sauce, water and ginger. Warm vegetable oil in a wok over medium heat. Add choy sum and stir-fry until slightly softened and color intensifies, about 3 minutes. Stir in fish sauce mixture and toss until choy sum is well coated. Cover and cook for 2 minutes. Serve hot.

SWEET-AND-SOUR POTATOES

SERVES 4

1 lb (500 g) uniformly sized desiree or pontiac
    potatoes, (about 3–4 medium)
salt as needed
3 tablespoons vegetable oil
1/2 teaspoon brown or black mustard seeds
36 fresh curry leaves
1/2 teaspoon ground turmeric
1/2 cup (4 fl oz/125 ml) coconut milk
1/4 cup (1/3 oz/10 g) chopped cilantro (fresh coriander)
4 teaspoons finely chopped fresh green chilies
1 teaspoon sugar
juice of 1 lemon

Place potatoes and large pinch salt in a
saucepan with enough cold water to cover.
Bring to a boil over medium–high heat.
Reduce heat to medium–low and cook,
partially covered, until potatoes are tender,
about 20 minutes. Drain potatoes and let
cool for 15 minutes. Peel potatoes and cut
into 1½-inch (4-cm) cubes. Set aside.

In a wok, heat oil over medium–low heat.
Add mustard seeds and cook until they
crackle, about 30 seconds.

Add curry leaves and turmeric and cook,
stirring, for 15 seconds. Add potatoes and
season with salt. Toss gently to combine.
Add coconut milk, cilantro, chilies and sugar,
and simmer, gently stirring occasionally, for
2 minutes. Drizzle with lemon juice and
serve hot.

Desserts

CREAM AND BERRY STACK

SERVES 4

vegetable oil, for deep-frying
8 wonton wrappers
8 oz (250 g) ricotta cheese
1/2 cup (4 fl oz/125 ml) heavy (double) cream
4 tablespoons confectioners' (icing) sugar, sifted
2 teaspoons Grand Marnier
1 teaspoon grated orange zest (rind)
5 oz (150 g) fresh raspberries
5 oz (150 g) fresh strawberries, hulled (stemmed) and sliced
3 oz (90 g) fresh blueberries

In a wok or frying pan, heat oil until it reaches 375°F (190°C) on a deep-frying thermometer or until a small bread cube dropped in oil sizzles and turns golden. Working in batches, add wonton wrappers and fry until golden on both sides, about 1 minute. Using slotted spoon, remove from pan and drain on paper towels. Allow to cool.

In bowl, combine ricotta cheese, cream, 3 tablespoons of sugar, Grand Marnier and orange zest. Using electric mixer beat until light and fluffy, 2–3 minutes. Cover and chill until ready to serve.

In another bowl, combine raspberries, strawberries and blueberries. Cover and chill.

To serve, place one wonton on each plate. Spread with ricotta filling. Spoon berries over filling. Top with second wonton. Dust with some of the remaining sugar.

CREAMY COCONUT BLACK RICE

SERVES 4–5

1 cup (7 oz/220 g) black sticky (glutinous) rice
1 cup (8 fl oz/250 ml) cold water
1½ cups (12 fl oz/375 ml) thin coconut cream
    or coconut milk
⅓ cup palm or brown sugar
2 teaspoons grated lime or lemon zest (rind)
pinch salt
1 cup (8 fl oz/250 ml) thick coconut cream (optional)
1 medium (12 oz/375 g) mango, peeled and sliced,
    for serving

Place rice in a bowl and add cold water to
cover. Let soak overnight, drain, and rinse well
under cold running water. Place rice and water
in a bowl that fits in a bamboo steamer or
steamer basket.

Partially fill a wok or pot with water
(steamer should not touch water) and bring
to a rapid simmer. Place steamer over water,
cover, and steam until rice is tender,
40–45 minutes, stirring occasionally. Remove
from heat and stir in thin coconut cream,
sugar, lime zest and salt. Cover and steam
until thickened to consistency of hot cereal,
15–20 minutes.

Swirl thick coconut cream through, if
desired, and serve with sliced mango.
Alternatively, cut a small cantaloupe
(rockmelon) in half, scoop out seeds, and fill
with rice.

FIG IN SYRUP

SERVES 6-8

1 lb (500 g) dried figs
4 cups (32 fl oz/1 L) cold water
1/3 cup (2 oz/60 g) whole blanched almonds
3/4 cup (6 oz/185 g) granulated sugar
thin strip lemon zest (rind)
juice of 1 lemon
3 tablespoons honey
chopped almonds, pistachios or walnuts, for garnish
whipped cream or plain (natural) yogurt, for garnish

Rinse figs well, place in a bowl and add cold water. Let stand for 8 hours until plump. Drain off water into a large wok.

Insert an almond into each fig from bottom. Set aside.

Add sugar to water in the wok and cook over medium heat, stirring occasionally, until sugar dissolves. Add lemon zest, juice and honey, and bring to a boil. Add stuffed figs and return to a boil. Reduce heat to low and cook, uncovered, until figs are tender and syrup is thick, about 30 minutes. Remove lemon zest and discard.

Arrange figs upright in a bowl. Pour syrup over figs, let cool, cover, and chill in refrigerator.

Sprinkle with chopped nuts and serve with whipped cream or yogurt.

PANFRIED PINEAPPLE

SERVES 4

6 oz (180 g) unsalted butter

1 small pineapple (about 1½ lb/750 g), peeled, cut
    lengthwise into quarters, cored and thinly sliced

¾ cup (5½ oz/165 g) packed brown sugar

¼ cup (2 fl oz/60 ml) dark rum or brandy

Melt butter in large frying pan over medium
heat. Add pineapple slices and cook for
1 minute. Sprinkle evenly with brown sugar
and cook, turning pineapple occasionally, until
sugar is melted and pineapple is translucent,
2–3 minutes. Add rum or brandy, stir to
combine and cook 1 minute.

To serve, place pineapple on plates and
spoon warm sauce over top

ROSE WATER DOUGHNUTS

MAKES 30 DOUGHNUTS

FOR YOGURT SAUCE
6½ oz (200 g) plain (natural) yogurt
3 teaspoons rose water
1 tablespoon confectioners' (icing) sugar, sifted

2¼ cups (11 oz/330 g) self-raising flour, sifted
½ cup (2 oz/60 g) ground almonds
⅓ cup (3 oz/90 g) butter or ghee, plus 2 cups
    (16 fl oz/500 ml) vegetable oil or ghee, for deep-
    frying
⅓ cup (3 fl oz/90 ml) plain (natural) yogurt
¼ cup (2 fl oz/60 ml) warm water
2 teaspoons rose water
grated zest (rind) of 1 orange
⅓ cup (2½ oz/75 g) superfine (caster) sugar

In a small bowl, combine yogurt, rose water and sugar. Mix well. Cover and refrigerate until ready to serve.

In a bowl, combine flour and almonds. Using fingertips, rub ⅓ cup (3 oz/90 g) butter or ghee into flour. Stir in yogurt, warm water, rose water and orange zest. Mix to form soft dough. Turn out onto floured work surface. Knead until smooth, about 2 minutes. Divide dough into 30 pieces. Roll each into ball.

In a wok, heat 2 cups (16 fl oz/500 ml) vegetable oil or ghee until it reaches 375°F (190°C) on a deep-frying thermometer or until a small bread cube dropped into liquid sizzles and turns golden. Working in batches, add doughnuts and deep-fry until golden, 5–6 minutes. Using slotted spoon, remove from wok and drain on paper towels. Place superfine sugar on plate and roll each doughnut in sugar until well coated.

Serve warm, with yogurt sauce.

SPICY FRUIT SALAD

SERVES 4

1¼ cups (10 fl oz/300 ml) water
½ cup (4 oz/125 g) decorating (crystal) sugar
juice and zest (rind) of 1 orange
3 star anise

6 whole black peppercorns
6 whole cardamom pods
3 cinnamon sticks
3 peaches, peeled, pitted and sliced
4 fresh figs, quartered
1½ cups (6½ oz/200 g) blueberries
2 oranges, peeled and cut into segments

In a wok, combine water, sugar, orange zest and juice, star anise, peppercorns, cardamom and cinnamon. Place over low heat and stir until sugar dissolves.

Raise heat to medium and bring to a boil. Reduce heat to low and simmer, uncovered, for 10 minutes. Remove from heat. Add peaches, figs, blueberries and oranges.

Allow to cool to room temperature and serve warm or refrigerate for 30 minutes and serve chilled.

SWEET DATE WONTON

MAKES 24 WONTONS

6½ oz (200 g) dates, pitted and chopped

½ cup (2 oz/60 g) walnuts, chopped

6½ oz (200 g) fresh or canned lychees, pitted
    and chopped

1 tablespoon grated orange zest (rind)

24 wonton wrappers

1 egg, beaten

vegetable oil, for deep-frying

2 tablespoons confectioners' (icing) sugar, sifted

In a bowl, combine dates, walnuts, lychees and orange zest. Mix well. Place wonton wrappers on work surface and cover with damp kitchen towel. Working with one wrapper at a time, lay on work surface and place 1 teaspoon filling in middle. Brush edges of wonton with egg, gather edges and twist to seal. Repeat with remaining wonton wrappers.

In a wok or frying pan, heat oil until it reaches 375°F (190°C) on a deep-frying thermometer or until a small bread cube dropped in oil sizzles and turns golden. Working in batches if necessary, add wontons and fry until golden, 1–2 minutes. Using slotted spoon, remove from pan and drain on paper towels. Allow to cool.

Sprinkled with confectioners' sugar and serve.

On the side

CHILI OIL

MAKES ABOUT 1 CUP (8 FL OZ/250 ML)

3/4 cup (6 fl oz/180 ml) vegetable oil

1/2 cup dried chili flakes

In a well-ventilated room, heat oil in a wok or small, heavy saucepan over medium to medium–high heat, just until surface shimmers. Add chili flakes. Stir briefly and immediately remove from heat. Let cool. If tightly covered, chili oil will keep indefinitely at room temperature.

GARLIC DIPPING SAUCE

MAKES ABOUT 1/2 CUP (4 FL OZ/125 ML)

3 tablespoons soy sauce

2 tablespoons Worcestershire sauce

1 tablespoon Asian sesame oil

4 cloves garlic, finely chopped

1 tablespoon superfine (caster) sugar

In a bowl, combine soy sauce, Worcestershire sauce, sesame oil, garlic and sugar. Stir until sugar dissolves. Cover and chill before serving.

FISH SAUCE WITH CHILIES

MAKES ABOUT 1 1/2 CUPS (12 FL OZ/375 ML)

1 cup (8 fl oz/250 ml) fish sauce

1 cup (5 oz/150 g) thinly sliced, fresh medium red or green chilies

cloves from 1/2 bulb garlic, finely chopped

2–3 tablespoons fresh lime juice to taste

In a small bowl or screw-top jar, combine all ingredients, stir or shake to blend, and serve. Refrigerate, covered, for several days.

Tip

This is the ubiquitous table seasoning of Thailand, used as commonly as salt and pepper. For a less spicy sauce, halve the chilies lengthwise and scrape away some or all of the seeds. Then thinly slice the chilies as above and continue.

HOT CHILI SAUCE

MAKES ABOUT 1 CUP (8 FL OZ/250 ML)

2 lb (1 kg) ripe tomatoes, quartered
3 small dried red chilies, split and seeded
4 tablespoons boiling water
1 tablespoon olive oil
1 onion, finely chopped
1 clove garlic, crushed
olive oil (optional)

Place tomatoes in heavy-bottomed saucepan over low heat and cook, stirring occasionally, until they break down and form sauce, about 1 hour. Add a little water if mixture begins to stick. Press through a sieve, set over bowl. (Do not use food processor, as skins need to be removed after tomatoes are cooked.) Set aside.

Place chilies in bowl, add boiling water and let stand 10 minutes. Remove from water and chop; reserve 1 tablespoon of water. Place chilies and reserved water in food processor and process until smooth. Set aside.

In a frying pan, warm oil over medium–high heat. Add onion and cook until softened, about 2 minutes. Add garlic and cook until aromatic, about 1 minute. Reduce heat to low and stir in chili purée. Add tomato pulp (with skins removed) and cook until thickened, about 5 minutes. Remove from heat and allow to cool.

Pour into airtight container and refrigerate until ready to serve. To store for up to 3 weeks, drizzle film of olive oil over top of sauce.

MANGO, PAPAYA AND GREEN CHILI RELISH

SERVES 4

1 small ripe mango, peeled, pitted and chopped

1/4 small papaya, peeled, seeded and chopped

1/2 long green chili, seeded and finely chopped

6 scallions (shallots/spring onions), sliced

1 kaffir lime leaf, finely shredded or 1/2 teaspoon grated lime zest (rind)

3 tablespoons fresh lime juice

2 teaspoons Asian sesame oil

In a small bowl, combine mango, papaya, chili, scallions and lime leaf. Stir in lime juice and sesame oil.

Mix well. Cover and chill for 30 minutes.

MINT RAITA

SERVES 8

1/2 cup (3/4 oz/20 g) coarsely chopped fresh mint

1/2 cup (3/4 oz/20 g) coarsely chopped cilantro (fresh coriander)

4 teaspoons finely grated fresh ginger

2 teaspoons finely chopped fresh green chili

1 cup (8 oz/250 g) plain (natural) whole-milk yogurt

salt to taste

In a food processor, combine mint, cilantro, ginger and chili and process until finely chopped.

In a bowl, whisk yogurt. Add chopped mint mixture and mix well. Season with salt.

Note: Raitas are based on yogurt, which is whipped or whisked. You can use either whole-milk (full-fat) or reduced-fat yogurt. This raita can be made 1 day ahead. Store in an airtight container in the refrigerator.

TAHINI SAUCE

MAKES ABOUT 1½ CUPS (12 FL OZ/375 ML)

2 cloves garlic
½ teaspoon salt, plus extra salt to taste
¾ cup (6 fl oz/185 ml) tahini
⅓ cup (3 fl oz/90 ml) cold water
⅓ cup (3 fl oz/90 ml) lemon juice

In a small bowl, crush garlic with ½ teaspoon salt and mix to a paste. Gradually add tahini, beating well with a wooden spoon.

Then alternately beat in small amounts of water and lemon juice. The water will thicken the mixture; lemon juice will thin it. Add all the lemon juice, and enough water to give the sauce a thin or thick consistency, depending on use. The flavor should be tart. Add salt to taste if necessary. Use the sauce as a dip with pita bread or as an accompaniment for falafel, fried or poached fish, or boiled cauliflower or potatoes.

Food processor method: Place tahini and garlic in processor bowl and process for a few seconds to crush garlic. Add lemon juice and water alternately, a small amount at a time, until desired consistency is reached. Blend in salt to taste.

SAMBAL OELEK

MAKES ABOUT 1½ CUPS (12 FL OZ/375 ML)

1 lb (500 g) red chilies
2½ cups water (20 fl oz/625 ml)
1 tablespoon white vinegar
1 teaspoon superfine (caster) sugar
2 tablespoons peanut oil
½ cup (4 fl oz/125 ml) boiling water

This mixture of red chilies, vinegar and salt is used throughout Asian cooking as a flavoring and as a spicy hot condiment.

Remove stems from chilies. Remove seeds if you want less fiery sambal oelek. Place chilies and water in a saucepan over medium heat and bring to a boil. Cover, reduce heat to simmer and cook until chilies are soft, about 15 minutes. Drain. Working in batches, place chilies in a food processor and process until smooth. Add vinegar, sugar, peanut oil and boiling water and process to combine. Pour into sterilized jars, seal and refrigerate for up to 1 month.

THAI CHILI DIPPING SAUCE

MAKES ABOUT 1 CUP (8 FL OZ/250 ML)

15 fresh long green chilies, roasted
1 whole bulb garlic
9 shallots (French shallots), about 3 oz (100 g),
     preferably pink
1/4 teaspoon dried shrimp paste
1/2 teaspoon salt
1 tablespoon fish sauce

Peel and stem the roasted chilies but retain
seeds. (For a less piquant sauce, discard some
or all of the seeds.) Preheat oven to 400°F
(200°C). Lightly break unpeeled garlic bulb by
pressing on a knife handle with the heel of
your hand, so that the cloves sit loosely
together; do not separate cloves from bulb
completely. Separately wrap the garlic and
shallots in aluminum foil. Roast on the top
shelf of the oven for about 30 minutes, or
until soft to touch. Remove from oven and
allow to cool to touch in foil. Peel shallots and
garlic (you should have about ⅓ cup (1½
oz/45 g) shallots).

In a mortar, pound chilies gently with a
pestle to break them up. Add garlic, and pound
briefly, then add shallots. Add shrimp paste and
salt and pound again to a coarse paste. Or
pulse ingredients in a food processor. Stir in
fish sauce. Serve with a selection of vegetable
crudités.

GLOSSARY

ASIAN SESAME OIL: Rich, dark- or golden-colored oil extracted from sesame seeds. Oil made from toasted seeds has a pronounced nutty flavor.

BAMBOO LEAVES: Long, narrow leaves available dried from Asian food stores. Leaves impart subtle flavor to food, but are not eaten. Soak briefly in boiling water to soften before use.

BAMBOO SHOOTS: Young shoots of a tropical plant, which are boiled to retain their sweet flavor. Most commonly found canned, packed in water.

BANANA LEAVES: Large leaves from the banana plant, used to line bamboo steamers or for wrapping foods prior to steaming. Parchment (baking) paper may be substituted. The leaves are available fresh or frozen.

BEAN SPROUTS: Sprouted beans and peas add a fresh flavor and crunchy texture to salads and other Asian dishes. Mung bean sprouts are sold fresh or canned. Snow pea (mange-tout) sprouts are available fresh. Fresh sprouts have a cleaner taste and crisper texture.

BOK CHOY: Asian variety of cabbage with dark green leaves and thick white stems. Sizes vary from baby bok choy about 6 inches (15 cm) long to bok choy as long as a celery stalk.

CHILI OIL: Spicy oil produced by steeping red chilies in oil. It is available bottled, or you can prepare your own (see page 85).

CHILI PASTE: Fiery condiment made from ground red chilies and sometimes garlic. Use in small quantities.

CHINESE BROCCOLI: Broccoli with white flowers and a bitter taste. Also known as gai laan. Sometimes confused with choy sum. Chinese broccoli and choy sum can be used in place of each other.

CHINESE CELERY: Straggly and sparse in appearance compared with standard celery, Chinese celery is also a darker green and more pronounced in flavor. Use both the stems and leaves.

CHINESE DRIED MUSHROOMS: Intensely flavorful, dark mushrooms that need to be rehydrated before use. The stems are discarded. Flavorful fresh mushrooms make an acceptable substitute.

CHOY SUM: Also known as flowering cabbage, this mild-flavored Chinese green has thin stalks bearing leaves and yellow flowers, all of which are used in cooking.

CUMIN: Also known as comino. The small crescent-shaped seeds have an earthy, nutty flavor. Available whole or ground.

FENUGREEK: The seed of an aromatic plant of the pea family, native to the Mediterranean region. Has a bittersweet, burnt sugar after-taste. Available whole or ground.

FISH SAUCE: Also known as nam pla, nuoc nam and patis, this distinctive, salty sauce is made from fermented shrimp or fish and is used similarly to soy sauce: to enhance and balance the flavor of dishes. Some are much saltier than others; use sparingly and add to taste.

FIVE-SPICE POWDER: This is made of an equal mixture of ground Szechuan peppercorns, star anise, fennel, cloves and cinnamon. Available at most supermarkets.

FLOWERING CABBAGE: See Choy sum.

GHEE: A form of clarified fat or pure butter fat, originating in India. Has a high smoke point and a nutty, caramel-like flavor.

GINGER: Thick rootlike rhizome of the ginger plant has a sharp, pungent flavor. Once the thin tan skin is peeled away from fresh ginger, the flesh is grated and used in sauces, marinades, stir-fries and dressings, or is sliced, bruised and added to stocks and soups. Store fresh ginger in refrigerator for 2–3 days.

KAFFIR LIME: The distinctive fragrant double leaves and fruit of this Asian tree are increasingly available fresh from Asian and many Western supermarkets. Frozen and dried leaves and frozen fruit are also available but lack the flavor of the fresh.

LEMONGRASS: A popular lemon-scented grass used in Asian-style dishes. Use only the white part or the bulb. Trim the root and remove the outer layer. Chop finely or bruise by hitting with a meat mallet or the blunt side of a chef's knife to bring out the flavor.

LONG BEAN: Related to the black-eyed pea, this thin, flexible but crisp-textured green bean is cut into short lengths before cooking. Long beans are also called snake beans and yard-long beans, though most found in markets are 24 inches (60 cm) or less in length.

MISO: Thick paste of fermented ground soybeans, used in Japanese soups and other dishes. Light-colored varieties of miso are milder in flavor than dark-colored pastes.

MIZUNA: A feathery Japanese salad green with a delicate flavor.

MUSHROOMS, TREE EAR OR CLOUD (BLACK OR WHITE FUNGUS): These add texture, but little taste, to food, but absorb flavors during cooking. The dried mushrooms must be soaked in water to rehydrate, then rinsed thoroughly and drained.

Trim the tough stems from the fresh or dried mushrooms before using.

NAM PLA: See Fish sauce.

OYSTER MUSHROOMS: Creamy white mushrooms with fanshaped caps, named for their resemblance to an oyster. Possessing a very mild, delicate flavor, oyster mushrooms grow in the wild and are cultivated. Available fresh in well-stocked supermarkets and produce markets. Replace with button mushrooms if unavailable.

SAMBAL OELEK: Indonesian paste consisting of ground chilies combined with salt and occasionally vinegar. This spicy condiment is available bottled, or you can prepare your own (see page 88).

SHISO: Aromatic green, jagged-edged leaf from the perilla plant, which is part of the mint and basil family. Shiso leaves are used in salads, cooked dishes such as tempura, and as a garnish. Shiso leaves are available fresh from Asian markets.

SHRIMP PASTE: Produced by drying, salting and pounding shrimp into a pungent-flavored paste that is then formed into blocks or cakes.

SOY SAUCE: Salty sauce made from soybeans and used both as an ingredient and as a table condiment. Dark soy sauce, usually used in cooking, is thicker and often less salty than light soy sauce, which is added to dipping sauces. Low-sodium products are also available.

STAR ANISE: The dried eight-pointed star-shaped seed pod of a tree belonging to the magnolia family. Star anise is one of the ingredients of Chinese five spice powder. It is also used whole, in segments or ground in Asian cooking. It has an intense liquorice flavor.

SWEET CHILI SAUCE: A mild chili sauce, used as a dipping sauce or combined with other sauces, such as soy, plum or ketjap manis. May also contain garlic and/or ginger. Hotter and less-sweet chili sauces may be substituted.

TAMARIND PULP: Available as powder, paste or pulp, this popular Asian fruit adds a sour flavor. Soak pulp required in hot water for about 15 minutes, then push through a fine-mesh sieve to extract the liquid, discarding the pulp. Dissolve powders and pastes before use, but be aware that some can be quite salty.

TOFU: Produced from soybeans that have been dried, soaked, cooked, puréed and pressed to form cakes or squares that range in texture from soft to firm. Mild in flavor, tofu readily absorbs the seasonings of the preparations in which it is used.

TURMERIC: A dried, powdery spice produced from the rhizome of a tropical plant related to ginger. It has a strong, spicy flavor and yellow color. Also known as Indian saffron.

INDEX

WEIGHTS AND MEASUREMENTS

The conversions given in the recipes in this book are approximate. Whichever system you use, remember to follow it consistently, to ensure that the proportions are consistent throughout a recipe.

Weights

Imperial	Metric
$1/3$ oz	10 g
$1/2$ oz	15 g
$3/4$ oz	20 g
1 oz	30 g
2 oz	60 g
3 oz	90 g
4 oz ($1/4$ lb)	125 g
5 oz ($1/3$ lb)	150 g
6 oz	180 g
7 oz	220 g
8 oz ($1/2$ lb)	250 g
9 oz	280 g
10 oz	300 g
11 oz	330 g
12 oz ($3/4$ lb)	375 g
16 oz (1 lb)	500 g
2 lb	1 kg
3 lb	1.5 kg
4 lb	2 kg

Volume

Imperial	Metric	Cup
1 fl oz	30 ml	
2 fl oz	60 ml	$1/4$
3 fl oz	90 ml	$1/3$
4 fl oz	125 ml	$1/2$
5 fl oz	150 ml	$2/3$
6 fl oz	180 ml	$3/4$
8 fl oz	250 ml	1
10 fl oz	300 ml	$1^1/4$
12 fl oz	375 ml	$1^1/2$
13 fl oz	400 ml	$1^2/3$
14 fl oz	440 ml	$1^3/4$
16 fl oz	500 ml	2
24 fl oz	750 ml	3
32 fl oz	1L	4

Oven temperature guide

The Celsius (°C) and Fahrenheit (°F) temperatures in this chart apply to most electric ovens. Decrease by 25°F or 10°C for a gas oven or refer to the manufacturer's temperature guide. For temperatures below 325°F (160°C), do not decrease the given temperature.

Oven description	°C	°F	Gas Mark
Cool	110	225	$1/4$
	130	250	$1/2$
Very slow	140	275	1
	150	300	2
Slow	170	325	3
Moderate	180	350	4
	190	375	5
Moderately hot	200	400	6
Fairly hot	220	425	7
Hot	230	450	8
Very hot	240	475	9
Extremely hot	250	500	10

Useful conversions

$1/4$ teaspoon	1.25 ml
$1/2$ teaspoon	2.5 ml
1 teaspoon	5 ml
1 Australian tablespoon	20 ml (4 teaspoons)
1 UK/US tablespoon	15 ml (3 teaspoons)

Butter/Shortening

1 tablespoon	$1/2$ oz	15 g
$1^1/2$ tablespoons	$3/4$ oz	20 g
2 tablespoons	1 oz	30 g
3 tablespoons	$1^1/2$ oz	45 g

Published in Australia in 2004 by
Lansdowne Publishing Pty Ltd
Level 1, 18 Argyle St
The Rocks, Sydney, 2000

Created and produced by Lansdowne Publishing
Text: Robert Carmack, Soon Young Chung, Didier Corlou, Shunsuke Fukushima, Ajoy Joshi,
   Vicki Liley, Tess Mallos, Sompon Nabnian, Jan Purser, Suzie Smith, Brigid Treloar, Nguyen Thanh Van
Photographers: Alan Benson, Ben Dearnley, Vicki Liley, Louise Lister, Andre Martin
Designer: Avril Makula
Editor: Joanne Holliman
Production Manager: Sally Stokes
Project Co-ordinator: Kate Merrifield

National Library of Australian Catologing-in-Publication Data
Stir fries.
   Includes index.
   ISBN 1 86302 822 6.
   1. Stir frying.
   641.774

Set in Meta Plus and Bembo on QuarkXPress
Printed in Singapore by Tien Wah Press